SECRETS OF LOOKING YOUNGER

7 practical steps on how you can make your face completely wrinkle and acne free

BY

LUCY MADISON

DISCLAIMER

Everything stated in this report is provided solely for your information and should not be taken as a medical instruction. It is advised that if any action or inaction should be taken, it should not be based solely on the contents of this book; instead, readers should consult with the appropriate health practitioners on any matter that pertains to their well-being and health.

The opinions and information given in this book are believed to be based on the best judgment of the author, and the readers who decide not to seek advice from the appropriate health authorities or professionals assume the risk of any complications that may arise.

TABLE OF CONTENTS

INTRODUCTION

Maintaining a clear and clean skin devoid of wrinkles and acne is paramount. When this is achieved, you tend to look younger and be admirable by everyone. Acne is one of the skin diseases that disfigure the face and other parts of the body.

Sometimes, acne can be very complex and could be a pointer to some problems in the body, like poor digestion, liver problems, blood toxins and colon problems.

Most of the routine treatments of acne comprise of reducing the hormones of the body, attacking the bacteria that causes acne or unclogging the pores of the skin. There are also medical creams, potions and pills used to treat acne. But this book will try to reveal the secret tips to treat acne that doctors usually necessarily don't talk about. You will learn ways to treat pimples in a more natural way.

THE METHODS REVEALED IN THIS BOOK WILL ALSO WORK FOR YOU IF YOU DESIRE A GLOWING AND WRINKLE FREE SKIN. THE HOMEMADE MASKS AND OTHER METHODS WILL DEFINITELY ADDRESS THIS.

ANATOMY OF THE SKIN

The largest organ in the body is the skin. It helps in getting rid of the waste products produced by the elimination organs of the body (mainly the liver and the kidneys).

It has two layers: the epidermis and the dermis.

The epidermis is the uppermost layer which in turn has 5 different layers.

The dermis is below the epidermis. The dermis contains sweat glands, sebaceous glands, nerves, hair follicles, and lymphatic vessels. The dermis also contains collagen fibres and elastin which helps the skin to be firm and flexible.

The fat cells (also called adipose tissues) are found under the dermis.

BRIEF TALK ABOUT ACNE

Acne also called Pimples, also known as acne vulgaris, is a common skin disease that usually affects the skin on the face, back, shoulders and chest.

It is a condition in which sebum is excessively secreted, and the hair follicles are inflamed.

A disorder in which there is excessive secretion of sebaceous gland and inflammation in hair follicles which is dependent on the presence of circulating androgenic hormones.

Pimple treatment is important because of some complications that are associated with it if poorly managed.

TYPES OF ACNE

Acne vulgaris: this is the commonest type of acne. It can be divided into closed comedo known as (whiteheads) and open comedo (known as blackheads). The blackheads are formed as result of pressing the whiteheads, which eventually leaves a dark spot on the face.

Acne conglobata: This is one of the severest forms of acne. It is commoner among men and is usually found around the face, back and chest. It forms nodules and multiple cysts.

Acne rosacea: one main feature of this is the characteristic flushed appearance of the face which is as a result of the blood vessels that are enlarged due to inflammatory bumps. It is commonly found on the forehead and the chin.

Perioral dermatitis: It commonly presents as tiny papules around the mouth and chin. Young women usually are victims of this type of acne.

HOW COMMON IS ACNE?

It is very common, especially during adolescence: Worldwide data has shown that it is seen in both sexes when they reach puberty with some variations in the tropics.

Not so common in later life

HOW IS ACNE FORMED?

It exists in areas of the body with the highest concentration of sebaceous glands, and these areas appear to be extremely sensitive to small quantities of androgens. There are four factors contributing to the formation of acne. These are;

1. **Excessive production of Sebum:** this occurs when male hormones called androgens that circulate

in the blood stream are produced excessively. These hormones make the sebaceous gland to produce large amounts of sebum.

2. Abnormal follicular differentiation: this leads to blockage of the pores.

3. Bacterial colonization: excessive production of sebum, certain blood toxins, and clogged pores create a conducive environment for acne bacteria (which is called *Propionibacterium acnes*)

4. Inflammation: when bacteria multiply, immune system is stimulated to produce some hormones called cytokines, which in turn produce an inflamed comedo in the sebaceous unit.

Being equipped with the knowledge of how acne forms, we now know what to do to stop it.

During ovulation, the ovaries secrete some androgen-like hormones, which cause the unique flare of acne at the time of menses. Oestrogens usually suppress the sebaceous gland and diminish the acne. This is why some people have acne when they ovulate and it disappears afterwards.

The blockage of hair follicles makes the sebaceous gland to distend, and form white heads in the skin. How severe acne will be, depends on the production of sebum; the more the production of sebum, the more severe the acne will be.

The inflammation is as a result of the proliferation of the 'acne bacteria' known as Propionibacterium acnes.

WHAT CAUSES OF ACNE?

- Puberty: This is usually as a result of the high level of testosterone produced during this stage of development; this increases production of sebum in the skin, making the skin to be greasy. The Sebaceous gland in the skin produces sebum which is a lipid rich substance.

- Premenstrual hormonal changes; this is why some women have acne just before their menses, as explained earlier.

- Heredity: It can be familial (especially if both parents have acne)

Other causes may include

- some disease entities like polycystic ovarian syndrome and Cushing's syndrome.

- Oily cosmetic products, drugs such as anabolic steroids, steroid creams and ointment, and lithium can also predispose people to have acne.

ACNE CAN BE A POINTER TO SOMETHING DANGEROUS GOING ON IN THE BODY

Enough said about acne. Now, let's look into what can be done to achieve or maintain a smooth face which can help you to look younger. These methods will also work for acne thereby helping us to have a body devoid of acne or spots. These are practical steps that if you follow them, you will achieve great results.

NATURAL WAYS TO ACHIEVE A SPOTLESS FACE AND ALSO GET RID OF ACNE

TIP 1. USE OF HOMEMADE MASKS

A. ONION AND OATMEAL MASK

Many people do not know that onion is very useful in making the face glow and spotless, and minimize wrinkles. It can also be used for the removal of acne and other scars from the face. However, the smell is pungent, and therefore can turn you off. This type of mask is one of the most effective methods.

How to make it: The ingredients you will use are included in the name of the mask: oatmeal and honey **(optional)**.

Cook half of a cup of pure oatmeal and allow it to cool. Afterward, peel one of the onions you got, and blend it till it becomes a puree. Add the puree to the oatmeal you had already cooked. If you notice that the mixture is not thick enough, you can apply pure honey to make it thick.

Apply to your face and leave it there for ten to fifteen minutes, after which you can slowly rinse it off.

If you are unable to finish the whole paste, the rest can be put inside refrigerator. It will still be good for use within 5 to 7 days.

B. EGG MASK

Ingredient: Raw Egg White.

How to make it: Break the egg and separate the yolk (the yellow part) from the white (the jelly like part).

Thereafter, whip the egg white until you have something that looks like a dense paste.

If you have an oily skin, you can put some lemon juice into the paste and mix them together. Apply the mask and allow it to remain on your face for about 15 minutes.

After fifteen minutes, you can wash it off with cloth and warm water.

This is also one of the very effective masks that I know.

C. Yogurt Mask

Ingredients: With this type of mask, you only natural yogurt and pure honey. It is very easy to make.

How to make it: A teaspoon of honey and natural yogurt

Take one teaspoon of honey and heat it till it melts. Thereafter, mix the honey with a table spoon of yogurt that has medium fat content. Stir the ingredients together at room temperature and put it on the on your face. Let it be there for about thirty minutes. After thirty minutes, use cloth to wash it away. If this works for you, you can continue to use it for like 4 times a week. It makes skin glow and acne free. Don't forget, honey has antibacterial and hygroscopic properties.

D. Salt Mask

One of the simplest masks to make at home is the salt mask. **Ingredients:** Everything you need can be got at home - cooking salt and water

How to make it: Put some salt in water for about twenty minutes and put it on your face including acne spots, if you have and let it be there for fifteen to thirty minutes.

E. BAKING SODA MASK

This mask is not only easy to make, it can also work wonders on acne, and also remove spots and wrinkles, thereby making your very attractive and fresh.

Ingredients: You only need baking soda and water.

How to make it: Add little water to the baking soda and mix till you make a paste out of it. Apply on the face and acne spots.

Leave for a while to dry while you engage yourself in some house chores, and rinse it off. It can stay on your face for as long as you want, but let it be for at least 30 minutes.

The result can vary, depending on the type of skin you have.

TIP 2: VITAL VITAMINS AND MINERALS

The number of servings of fruits and vegetables recommended per day is three to five; however, most people don't take up to that.

Minerals and vitamins are trace elements which help the body to function properly, and the deficiency leads to some malfunction in the body. They can be taken in form of pills, especially if the consumption in food is lacking, however, they cannot be substituted for healthy food (balanced diet). Also too much of vitamins and minerals are not advisable as it could be dangerous to the health.

So, we will be discussing the recommended vitamins and minerals.

Vitamin A: this vitamin helps to stimulate the growth of healthy skin and eyes. They are also employed in the treatment of pimple and other skin diseases.

Carrots, tomatoes, pumpkin, citrus fruits like oranges are very good sources of vitamin A.

Vitamins E and C: these are vitamins with powerful antioxidant properties and are good for healthy skin. Vitamin C is especially known as the most important anti-acne vitamin.

If you take vitamins E and A, you should consider taking zinc supplement along with them, as Zinc helps in the proper absorption of vitamin A and also keeps the level of the vitamin stable in the blood.

Vitamin B6: It is also known as pyridoxine. Usually, inflamed skin is probably as a result of deficiency of vitamin B6. This condition can also be found in the alcoholics and aging adults.

Minerals that will help you keep a glowing skin devoid of wrinkles and acne include zinc, selenium and magnesium. We will take a look at them one after the other.

Zinc: This is a wonderful mineral that is beneficial in different ways. There are growing evidences that zinc is beneficial in the treatment of acne and also helps in slowing the process of aging, thereby giving you a glowing skin. It helps to have a healthy skin, and offers protection against ultraviolet light. It is also involved and important in the process of wound healing. It improves the immunity of an individual and also contributes to mental function. Another function of zinc is that it reduces the risk of some cancers and heart diseases. Sources of zinc include legumes (like beans, lentils, chickpeas), nuts, eggs, meat and so on.

Other minerals that should be taken seriously include selenium and magnesium. They are trace elements that have been found to fight acne and protect the skin from ageing as well. Selenium has been said to improve the elasticity of the skin while magnesium helps to balance the hormones, thereby reducing the effect of hormonal cycles of pimples.

Green leafy vegetables such as swish chard, collard greens, or baby spinach are very rich sources of magnesium.

Fruits, vegetables, yoghurt and milk are fantastic sources of selenium.

TIP 3: EXCELLENT FOODS TO EAT, ONE FORM OF WATER TO DRINK, AND FOODS TO AVOID

You want to maintain a clear, glowing and youthful skin; you should try these five excellent foods. These are seeds, zinc, water, raw foods and essential oils.

A. Raw foods and fresh juice

This is one thing that can give glowing and youthful skin, devoid of rashes, acne and eczema if taken for a month. Fresh foods and vegetables juices can work marvelously in keeping glowing and clear skin.

B. Zinc, Pumpkin seeds and Shellfish

As it was mentioned earlier, zinc helps in the repair of skin and also helps the skin to regenerate from scratches, cuts and scrapes. Shell fish and Pumpkin seeds are good food one can eat to be fresh.

C. Omega 3 oils

These oils are known for reducing inflammation and are natural, safer and cheaper than both steroids and non steroidal anti-inflammatory drugs. The ocean derived omega 3s are more effective than the ones derived from plants like chia seeds. They boost immune system, nervous system, heart functions and other bodily functions including brain and moods. Fishes are very good sources of omega 3.

C. Clean water

One of the things that are commonly overlooked in having healthy skin is hydration. Many people look older than their age with marked and wrinkled skin because they are dehydrated. It is important to drink at least eight glasses of water each day to have a healthy skin. This is commonly overlooked, but it is very important.

TIP 4: FOODS YOU SHOULD AVOID

- Fried foods

- Carbonated drinks

- Dead, frozen and processed foods including junk foods, processed meats, and unsaturated fats like margarine.   In some people, avoiding junk foods alone can help them conquer acne and other problems of the skin.

- Avoid pharmaceuticals

- Avoid milk and dairy products (including chocolate): many of the milk from cows and other dairy products like butter, cheese, and ice cream contain steroids which upset the bodies' hormonal balance.

TIP 5: IMPORTANCE OF GARLIC

Garlic has been known for centuries, for its antibacterial and healing properties. It has a substance called allicin; this is gotten when garlic is crushed or chopped, and it is useful in boosting immunity and fighting against acne and eventually helps to have a spotless skin.

Garlic has many benefits, and these benefits are gotten when it is crushed, cut, chopped and processed. Allicin, as one of the compounds found in garlic, has a very high sulphur content which made garlic to be used as antiviral, antibacterial and antifungal.

Below are some of the advantages that garlic provides:

- It boost the immune system
- It fights against fungal overgrowths

- It helps to reduce cholesterol

- It kills viruses and parasites

MORE ABOUT ALLICIN

In this section, we want to look at how allicin helps to fight against bacteria that cause skin diseases including acne.

As said earlier, when you chop or shred garlic, allicin is released, and it is the one that gives garlic its characteristic smell.

When garlic is eaten, allicin is carried around in the blood stream, and gets into the body and sweat.

So, when you sweat, the garlic assists in treating acne all day long. As an antibacterium, allicin will help to destroy the bacteria (propioniobacterium) that makes pimples to get inflamed.

Let me quickly show you a recipe you can try out if you don't mind to chew raw garlic.

- Cut three garlic cloves into pieces and put them in a bottle that contains some water. To make the taste friendly, you can add some lemon juice or any form of juice. Thereafter, drink from the bottle all the day. Do this every day, and you will be amazed at how you will have a fresh skin without wrinkles, and if you have acne, the acne will disappear.

TIP 6: HOME REMEDIES FOR SMOOTH FACE

These are little things we do not pay attention to, especially concerning hygiene that go a long way in maintaining a clear face devoid of acne and other forms of spots.

In this section, we will take a look at them.

1. Change your pillow case frequently

If pillow cases are not changed frequently, there will be build up of dirt, oils and bacteria, which is not a good thing for your face. Pillow cases should be changed once or twice per week if you desire a skin without spot, especially if you have acne. When you start, you may feel it is not making much effect, but over time, you will see real difference.

2. Reduce how many times you touch your face especially when you have pimple

We all touch our faces when we have pimple, and the truth is, it is not possible not to touch it. However, the touching can be limited. All these little things help in keeping a clean skin, and also help to eliminate acne.

3. Sleep on your back:

This is simple but weird. Sleeping on your abdomen makes your face to be in the pillow. If you desire a face free of acne, you should try sleeping on your back or side. This way, your face is not buried into the pillow, and will not get sweaty.

IF ALL THESE DO NOT WORK FOR YOUR ACNE, YOU MAY WANT TO TRY DETOXING AND COLON CLEANSING. MANY PEOPLE HAVE REPORTED PERMANENT RESULTS WITH THESE METHODS. APART FROM BEING FREE OF PIMPLES, OTHER ORGANS IN THEIR BODIES, LIKE LIVER, DIGESTIVE SYSTEMS AND KIDNEYS WORK OPTIMALLY.

TIP 7: Other tips for those that have acne

1. Try to reduce stress.

I am sure you are wondering how stress is related to acne. Stress can start acne and acne can lead to psychological stress. I will explain.

When we are stressed up or tensed, our body reacts by secreting steroid hormones like cortisol, and this causes a rise in the production of skin oils, leading to break out of the skin.

Now, when there is something called body-mind medicine. This means there is a way mind controls what an individual feels in the body and vice versa.

One of the complication of acne is psychological problems, for example, acne may make an individual to lose his/her self confidence.

When acne is much, the individual starts thinking of different problems pertaining to their looks, and this inturn causes psychological stress. And once acne is treated and it improves, the individual starts getting better mentally as well.

So, one of the ways to minimize acne is to reduce stess.

Learn some relaxation techniques like yoga, meditation, biofeedback and taichi.

2. Exercise Regularly: The importance of regular exercise cannot be overemphasized as well. You can do moderately exercise three to five times per day for 30 to 45 minutes. It will help you not only to tackle acne, but also to maintain your weight.

3. Stop Smoking.

SUMMARY AND CONCLUSION

I am sure that one way or the other; you have learnt valuable things in this write-up.

Information without action is nothing.

I will like you to act on the knowledge you have and you will be amazed how you will get results.

Make use of any of the various masks explained above, eat balanced diet, take a lot of fruits and vegetables, exercises your body well and drink at least 2 to 3 liters of clean water per day.

Put all these to actions and you will get good results.

Once again, thank you for buying this book.